Part 1
Expect The Unexpected

When You Least Expect it, People Do Extraordinary Things
A Knight In Shining Cab Armor

"Next" the underpaid, over-hassled, airline-agent, barked.

"ID?"

I reached into my bag for my wallet. I had intended to get it out before I got to the front of the line, but miracle of miracles...there was no line! I looked in the pocket, where it should go, and rarely is. The next pocket, and the next. I found nothing but the usual junk that collects in a black hole. No aluminum case, no driver's license, no credit card to pay for my luggage, no picture of my son! Nothing.

My nerve endings suddenly pulsed, like I had just put my hand into a giant electrical socket.

"Take your luggage off the scale and step aside please" the agent snipped.

"Oh, yes, the rewards of being a billion miler," I quipped.

Silence. A glare. Dismissal.

I hauled my luggage off the scale, struggling to slow the blood pounding in my ears. I tried to go to a quiet place in my head. (Not an easy task.) I retraced my steps, rewound my brain's videotape, and watched.

In the back seat of the taxi, I pulled out my wallet to pay for the cab. My colleague said, no, that he would pay. I was tired, really tired, and I put my wallet back into the outside pocket and did not zip it! I meant to. I always mean to. But I was listening to my friend. And my husband would tell you I am an expressive personality who defies order. (He's right, by the way.)

In my mind's eye, I could see my pink aluminum, keep-your-credit-cards-safe, wallet laying on the back seat of the taxi. No driver's license, no money! No go home.

Then I remembered that I had my ever-ready-to-travel passport, found my colleague, and leaned on him for bag fees. He is truly a mensch.

The search, for one cab amid thousands, began. My colleague helped. We tried to remember the slogan, its signs, and its color. What company was it? I began calling cab companies hoping to find my wallet, having zero expectations.

Ever tried to get a taxi on the street in DC? Getting a human to answer the phone is the same.

I left plaintive messages. Calls of distress, laden with, "It had my son's picture in it," pleas. Reality set in. I would never see the wallet again. We had a tasteless dinner, at a tasteless airport restaurant, and I tastelessly had to let my colleague pay.

"Cancel" "Confess" and Re-issue" ran through my head like a courtroom verdict. Plus, this incident was further proof that I need to be more organized. Apologizing to my colleague, once again, I imagined I heard someone say my name. "Did you hear that? My name?"

He looked at me with pity. There it was again, "Connie Timpson" come to the information desk.

Weaving through the crowd, like an doctor running to an injured person, I saw the most extraordinary thing – our cabbie, rushing towards me waving my pink aluminum wallet! I could not believe my eyes. He had indeed fixed my injury.

This extraordinary man was finished with his shift, yet when he found my wallet, he doubled back, parked, and braved the airport crowd to give it back to me.

I thanked him, and thanked him, and thanked him. I couldn't help it, I threw my arms around him and squeezed. Then I opened my wallet and gave him a big tip. Later I thought – not big enough, not nearly.

This cab driver could have kept it all, sold the credit cards, slipped the money into his wallet, and tossed the rest of my life into the trash. But he did not.

He showed me once again that there is "extraordinariness" in every one of us, and he let his "extraordinary" shine.

My assessment of him one hour earlier was that he was a pleasant and patient taxi driver from somewhere in North Africa. He was so much more - he is an extraordinary human being! A knight in shining cab armor

The extraordinary in all of us is just under the surface. All you have to do is listen, observe, and expect the unexpected. Expect the unexpected, because people do the unexpected. Look for the extraordinary in others, and explore your own extraordinariness. Yes, you've got it!

"Extraordinary" More Interesting Than "Famous"

When people learn that I am a former journalist many ask, "Who is the most famous person you have ever met?" I always hesitate, because "famous" is not important to me at all. It is true, that some famous people I have met and interviewed are also extraordinary, and I celebrate those people; like President Jimmy Carter, Benazir Bhutto, Johnny Cash and June Carter, Lakota Olympiad, Billy Mills, Sting, and others.

The better question is – *who is the most extraordinary person you have ever met?* Ah…there are many. Most of them humble-risk takers, blind to their exquisite gifts. They do not realize that they are extraordinary, or if they have a hint that they may be able to do something that no one else can, they are very quiet about it. Unless you ask – *they won't tell.*

CONNIE TIMPSON

Nah, It Ain't Nothin Special
A Humble Master Craftsman

We came to hear Geechee or Gullah, the nearly extinct language, born of slavery. Taken captive, from different African countries, slaves created the language as a way to communicate amongst themselves, to tell stories, share secrets, and plan escapes from their lives of misery. Mixing African, English, French and Portuguese, this creative blend of languages, provided a cloak of protection for the lips that spoke it. The man with the whip - frustrated, but none the wiser

As we stepped onto Sapelo, a barrier island off the coast of Georgia, we were seduced by the laid back rhythm of the island. Nothing, or no one, is in a hurry to go anywhere, or do anything on this island.

We rented the only possibility for transportation on the island, an almost dead, just-roll-the-windows-down-for-a little-relief-from-the-heat, 1960 Ford station wagon.

We nearly drowned in waves of silt as we choked our way towards what we learned was a family that had descended from slavery, and spoke the melodic old language.

The car stalled in the silt and we walked a mile or more through brushy marshland that we were later told had a "few varmints" we were lucky not to have met.

We are nosy journalists, so yes, we just showed up,

A man, worn smooth by some of life's most punishing seas, sat in a lawn chair weaving an intricate basket from Sweet Grass that grows over much of the island. We introduced ourselves and told him we wanted to know more about the Gullah language and hear it spoken. He threw his head back and laughed, then shook his head and muttered ummm…ummm…ummm. We prodded him.

James Green walked us back through history, first in the language of his people, then translating, as his fingers worked the design in the grass to the cadence of this melodic language.

His words were beautiful, but his hands hypnotic.

I couldn't keep my eyes off of them.

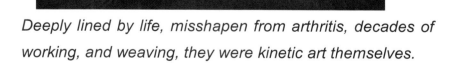

Deeply lined by life, misshapen from arthritis, decades of working, and weaving, they were kinetic art themselves.

As he told the old stories he created art as if he was listening to inner whispers, a collective memory spanning generations that worked the grass with him.

He caught my watchful eye, winked, shook his sweet grass creation, and said it was nothing special.

It was just one of those things his grandpa taught him to do, he told me. And like his grandfather, he taught his own grandchildren. Some were more interested than others, he said with a chuckle, and added that his basket weaving, gave him a little spending money.

My wallet flew out of my bag. I wanted a piece of artistry created by those magnificent hands, which seemed to tell stories as he turned sweet grass into art. I bought, and now cherish one of his creations.

I took pictures, (after his wife ran in to put on her best Sunday wig) and kept questioning this piece of living history. I told him that we would like to write an article about him, the Gullah language, and his stunning creations. Again, he said, "Nah…It ain't nothin special." I pushed.

His wife, also a weaver of these stunning creations, spoke for him.

"Sum a his stuff is in DC."

"Where?" I puzzled out loud, trying to figure out where her question would lead us.

"Let me show ya sumthin," she replied and scurried into the neatly cared for, little white clapboard house and returned with a newspaper clipping in her hand. My fingers met newsprint, so loved with time and touching, that it felt like baby powder in the palm of my hand. I looked down and my heart stopped.

In the photo, James Green stood with three of his extraordinary baskets, part of a permanent display in America's most prestigious museum.

"The Smithsonian!".
He repeated, "It's nothin."

YOU ARE EXTRAORDINARY!

To me, and my fellow journalist, this was SUMTHIN! This Gullah speaking man and his creations were EXTRAordinary.

This could have become a really good data story about the Gullah language and the people who speak it. When were the first slaves of the Gullah community brought to Sapelo? *1802.*

- How was the language created? *By combining several languages.*

- How many descendants remain on the island, and can speak the old language? *Fewer than 100.*

Important, information for historians, but the facts become almost irrelevant after you are invited to walk into the story of extraordinary people like this humble basket maker on Sapelo Island.

If we had not listened, watched, and explored, we would have seen this extraordinary person as part of America's shameful history. That would have been enough, but looking for more, just under the surface, we found an EXTRAordinary person.

There is an extraordinary person inside *you*. Yes, there is. You have a bit of talent, an extraordinary thought, a different way of looking at the world, a personality trait that sets you apart.

Look for it in others and you will more easily recognize it in yourself.

It is "sumthin."

You Too Are Extraordinary So is Your Story

Take a close look in the mirror. You have lived, breathed, used, taught, perfected, and inspired others. All of us have something that sets us apart, a talent, a bit of knowledge, the way we think, or the way we relate to others.

We have years of experience and have accumulated tons of inner wealth.

Extraordinary You

Like, James Greene, you may think what you know or do isn't anything out of the ordinary. But what may seem ordinary to you is, very likely, to be EXTRAordinary to others.

This humble artist left this world not too long after I met him, but his creations, his gift to the world will inspire others to keep the art, and his spirit alive. If we believe that every person possesses some extraordinariness – this world will be a better place.

I believe:

> **"Recognizing the extraordinariness in others helps us see the extraordinary in ourselves."**

Explore your own extraordinariness like you are searching for truffles. Root out the buried treasure and share. Each of us has strengths and gifts. Look beneath the packaging, the shiny wrapper. Explore the extraordinary within.

Beneath the Shiny Wrapper
Trekking to Extraordinary

Hiking on a narrow trail on the Pakistani side of the Himalayas, I rounded a corner and came full face with Pakistani mountain people. They were, like many mountain tribes, much larger than their city cousins. Only the women stayed on the path when they saw me. The men lowered their eyes and struck out through the brush. The women, whose faces were dark from campfire smoke, wore numerous handcrafted bangles and large earrings. Many had babies slung over their backs in colorful tribal cloths.

The Balti people are magnificent, and while I had no fear of them, I was a bit shy. They were curious, and as they passed me on the trail they touched my face, my arm, and giggled. I took no offense at being a "hands-on" exhibit to them, just as they were to me. Their touch, and curiosity, touched my soul.

We hiked higher, and higher, the beauty astounding. We were above the clouds at one point and I made the comment that I was Luke cloud Walker. We soon discovered, however, that getting above some of the clouds is not being above all clouds. We were not high enough to avoid what looked like a giant wall of water descending from the sky.

We began to descend, as quickly as possible, but the monsoon rains caught us, washing us off the trail and down the mountain. We were laughing, but the fact that we could not see our way off the mountain was inching up my spine, like a dead chill on a deserted street at night.

We had come to see the Rhesus monkeys, known locally as Bandar (Urdu). Now all I wanted to see was some kind of marking that would lead us back to where we left our jeep. We both knew we were in trouble, but neither of us said it. You know, it's that old, "If we don't say it, it isn't real" mentality?

Finally we saw a little wisp of smoke and worked our way towards it. Slogging in soaked shoes and clothes, we made our way to what we discovered was a small encampment.

As we approached, I saw the woman with the beautiful ring in her nose who had touched me on the trail hours earlier. She pointed at us and motioned for us to come her way. We did.

They fed us dal and chapatti cooked over the campfire. It was delicious. I will forever, hold this bit of human magic inside my heart.

After thanking our hosts, the women telling me shy goodbyes, with one last touch to my face that made them giggle. Two of the men guided us back to where our Jeep waited. Yes, I followed the men at a distance. Their culture differs greatly from my Western upbringing.

These people were extraordinary. They could have let us walk until we were completely lost, injured, or starved. Instead, they reached out to us.

I wish I had pictures, but that is something I knew they would not like. To this day, the image of the women on the trail comes back to me instantly when I think of good people.

When I use the word, Extraordinary, or hear words like monsoon, Himalayas, or monkeys I see those women, and that day.

My memory's snapshot is very clear.

If we open ourselves to seeing and experiencing the "Extraordinary" we will see it, and recall its images in the time it takes to snap a camera's shutter.

Doing "Nice" Does *Us* "Good"

Did you know that doing nice things for others boosts your serotonin levels? You may not care about knowing what a shot of serotonin does to the brain. You should, however, care about what raising your serotonin levels can do for you.

You might describe it as a "do good – feel good high".

Experts who study what serotonin does to the brain, say it really is the *happy hormone*. *The things we can learn from watching children!*

Dr. Lara Honos-Webb explains, "Serotonin is the neurotransmitter that gives us the feeling of satisfaction and well-being. Most of the anti-depressant medications work by increasing the amount of serotonin available to your brain."

It is a simple equation, with an empowering result.

> *"Doing good = elevated serotonin levels.*
>
> *Elevated serotonin levels = a happy brain*
>
> *A happy brain = a total "feel good" high*
>
> *(No running shoes required)*

All of this means that doing nice things for other people changes your brain in ways that make you feel better. It is one of the most beautiful equations on the planet –

Do good = Feel Good

I spend a lot of time in airports, so it is not surprising that some of my best and worst experiences have come from that connected, yet so unconnected, and impersonal world.

Rescuing Mom

Walking into the women's restroom, (not a place where conversation usually starts) I saw a mom struggling to change her kicking, screaming, flailing child. There was also a three-year-old hanging on her leg. She was on the verge of tears. No. She was in tears. I asked if I could help.

"I don't suppose you have a diaper," she replied with a hopeful smile, her chin quivering.

My son is grown. So no, I did not have a diaper, but I could help. Her 3 year old kept tripping on the paper towels he had wound around his feet. I leaned down and untangled him. Big mistake!

He bolted from the restroom and I ran after him. I returned with the 3 year old and told Mom to hang on, that I would find a diaper.

(Yes, I would have started asking moms with babies if they had a spare, if I had not found one in a gift shop.)

Diapers in hand I returned to Mom. While she changed the baby, I held out my arms to the 3 year old and told him I would help him wash his hands. We were old friends by now. Washed and dried, I offered to hold the baby, while Mom did the same.

Wow! The baby! I got to hold the baby! I love babies.

Mom washed her hands and then hugged me. Then the 3 year old hugged me. She offered to pay me.

No. It really was my pleasure to help. I zoomed to my plane, high on the serotonin created by this simple act of helping a Mom.

Really – I was helping me.

Doing good works wonders for the psyche!

Embrace Technology - *Don't Let It Blind You to the Extraordinary*

We have nearly lost the two most effective forms of communication – eye contact, and body language! We often miss the extraordinary when it happens right in front of us, because we are distracted by technology.

We have come to expect our best friend to text another friend while you try to tell her that you just got fired, or your husband just dumped you. She assures you that she is listening even though she is smirking at something another friend texted her.

Stay Connected 24/7 – whether you want to or not!

Technology has *connected more of us, but are we really communicating*?

Are we communicating, solving issues, trading and growing ideas? Or are we erecting barriers to clear communication? Are we using our *ability to connect* to document the fact that we "reached out" rather than "communicated"?

We sometimes say things in an email, or in a text that can be misconstrued, or that we don't dare say, or can't bring ourselves to say in person. Sometimes people say things in an email that can even get them fired, like three Iowa civil rights employees who sent gossipy, and demeaning emails about colleagues and management, calling one "Teen Wolf" another "Psycho."

Radio Shack told 400 workers that they were part of the workforce cutbacks...in an email. I'd say that is just a wee bit impersonal. And some people simply do not realize that what is said or shown in an email, text viral video, or anywhere else you can send digital information - is *permanent*.

What you say, and do on line, is not a big deal. Right? I mean, heck, who, and how, could anyone else find out? Oh, let me count the ways! Then begin counting the lost jobs, lawsuits, expensive breakups, and perhaps most of all - the meanness and humiliation.

Just ask former Congressman, Anthony Weiner, who was so taken with his own underwear image – that he shared it in the cyber world! It cost him his Congressional seat. The world's best golfer/husband/dad/role model, fell from dizzying heights when Tiger Wood's wife read his sexy texts to some of his sexiest "fans" and took a nine iron to his car. The list of "stupidity hall of fame" grew longer when retiring football legend, Brett Favre put himself on the list, by sharing naughty photos of himself with the ether. Their personal images are forever mired in Larry Flintish mud. If they could only take it back! But once it is out there, it's out there! Oops!

Take my mom's advice – "if you can't say it to their face – don't say it."

If you want your life to be private don't text it, sext it, tweet it, or write it and <u>DON'T</u> press SEND.

When you are reading about "tweets gone wrong" or are texting your BFF about the latest antics of your boss, you could be preparing your own pink-slip demise.

Worse, you are missing *real stuff.* Important stuff. If you are reading a screen you miss social cues, and communication that is vital to life.

Reading body language or looking someone in the eye helps you innately understand the emotion contained in the sub-text. Social cues are important in business. If we never learn how to read them, a face-to-face can be a disaster.

If you constantly have on headphones, one eye on text messages, the other on email – you can miss what could have been the most important exchange of your life. You could miss meeting extraordinary human beings.

If your *communication technology* is attached like an appendage, you won't see that the next Shell Silverstein is madly drawing characters on a sketchpad, while you are waiting in line at Starbucks.

You will not see the gleam of creativity in his or her eyes, nor will you see him drop a pencil that you could have retrieved. (You can write the rest of the story…)

Major corporations now recognize the *need to unplug from 24/7, cyber control.*

The German automaker Volkswagen now shuts down its email server 30 minutes after the workday ends, and only switches it on 30 minutes before work begins in the morning.

Ah…time to breath, create, think, or simply empty your head, so that when you switch it on, you really can – *switch it on. During the time technology is switched off, your people skills are open, your creative brain is more engaged and you are more open to explore and appreciate the world.*

CONNIE TIMPSON

Hiding Behind Technology

A few years ago I worked for a guy in an international start-up consulting firm, and because we each spent most of our waking hours running between airports, we sort of shared an office.

One day we are both in the office, both working, each facing a different wall. I am hammering away on a proposal, and I hear him say my name.

I answer, and turn to him, only to realize that while I am sitting only yards away, he is leaving me a voice mail!

I am still baffled by that one. Instead of discussing what he wanted to talk to me about, it took several exchanged voice mails, and a lot of "over thinking" to undertake and complete a very simple task.

We have all seen this one - the person who pretends to be talking on the cell phone, (or listening intently) so that he or she does not have to talk to, or communicate with anyone around her?

Smart phones give us an excuse to check out, form our own little cocoon of protection. I mean – someone could talk to me! How much of the world do they miss?

Are you letting technology put a barrier between you and others?

The most extraordinary person you could ever meet may be standing right in front of you, and you will not see him or her because you are hiding behind technology.

Taking a break during meetings rarely means "network" or exchange ideas, anymore. Instantly the Blackberry's, and I Phones appear. Check messages, send a text, but keep your eyes down. For the shy person – the smart phone is a dream come true, offering sanctioned behavior that wards off interaction with others.

Looking at words and symbols on a screen robs you of the opportunity to appreciate the *extraordinary* among us. If you cannot see or hear other people, if you are not "experiencing" the situation, you could miss one of the best moments of your life. Our world is filled with colorful, interesting people, and magical experiences.

In-Person Communication Forges Visceral Connections

Popping open my computer, I downed my first hit of hot coffee and nearly spewed it on the keyboard. It wasn't the hot coffee. It was - Northern Ireland and the IRA - once again in the news! This time it was a project of interviews done by Boston College.

The college promised to release the interviews only after the interviewees were dead. So much for promises. The secrets of the well-guarded project got whispered, heard, and went public. As Forbes Magazine put it – *the Belfast project* was to *recount* history, not *make* it.

Now the project, and its interviews, was making news. The whole thing fell into the gray zone – the foggy legal system of both countries. I was immediately transported to a Belfast where tanks and militia still controlled the streets.

BBC's Technology News 23 December 2011

The Child Storyteller Who Had No Childhood

I was consulting Ulster Television. 9/11 had not yet broken our hearts, but Belfast had lived that sort of terror for decades. The deadly struggles of North Ireland had long captured my attention, but not until I stepped foot on Belfast soil did I feel the palpable misery, mistrust, and uncertainty, that controlled it. I was shocked, when at the airport when I got 50 questions, then 50 more. It was like going to Israel.

Was I really who I say I am, who would I be working with? Names please. Where would I be staying? (That was code for "only some cab drivers" would take me to the hotel because it was in a "Catholic" area.)

After we were checked at the second roadblock, made to get out of the car and wait while it was examined and reexamined, we passed tanks, the cab driver mumbling "Bloody Brits" under his breath, while I gripped my seat and prayed!

He took me to the Europa Hotel – which holds the distinction of being the most bombed hotel in Europe. (The clerk gives you a paper signifying this fact when you check in.) I was not sure that was a recommendation, but it was interesting.

After a day of work with delightful people at Ulster, they took me out for supper, and a brew, at one of the world's most famous pubs – the Crown Bar. After we had downed a pint or two, the Ulster TV station manager (whose name has slipped into the – I really liked you but I can't remember your name file) motioned to someone to join us.

We moved into a sort of private area, with century old carved wood doors and stained glass windows, referred to as "snugs."

Within the walls of this, "snug", where I'm told many of Northern Ireland's "get-even plots" were born, I met the storyteller, Danny.

I was startled that he was in a pub at all.

Danny was a wee lad, skinny, his pants too short, and certainly not of drinking age. (I was further surprised when Danny downed the rest of a pint he held with a child's hand.) The whole picture was at odds with itself.

I asked his age, and he straightened his back and said, "Fourteen. A wee small for my age." Someone at the table whispered "eleven".

For a pound, he would tell me an Irish tale that would tickle my toes. Since hearing stories that tickle my toes, is one of my favorite things to do, I plunked down a pound and entered the world of Ulster fairy tales.

In an exaggerated Northern Ireland brogue, Danny told me, a very rich woman was carding wool when she heard a knock at the door. (He knocked on the door of the snug.) Supposing it was a neighbor she opened the door, and to her surprise in walked a woman who was also carding wool. The difference was not that she was faster or better, it was the one big horn, growing out the center of her head. (Everything Danny said, was in a different voice, and every movement pantomimed.)

Before it was all over Danny played out the lure of dragons, dragging giant claws across the table, jumping aside to avoid the fire coming from their noses, and taking a jab at them with his golden sword. There were fairies and tricksters, Kings and dungeons, knights and ladies, but most of all there were fire-breathing dragons.

Danny read our physical and emotional responses, and played on them. He was good! Really good. Delivering his last line, he pulled off his cap and bowed. I greedily plunked down another pound.

While it was great fun for me, it was anything but that for Danny. Sure, he liked telling stories, making people laugh, but storytelling was serious business for him. I learned that each coin he earned meant life for his family. He was a Catholic, the only boy in a house of eight girls. His father and older brother had been killed in the "Troubles of Northern Ireland". At eleven Danny was the man of the house. That was the real Northern Ireland.

The night wound down and I crossed the street to my very pleasant hotel, where I threw open the drapes only to discover there were no lights on this side of the hotel. Now that was odd.

I groped for what I thought must be a black out drape – it was plywood, placed there from the latest bomb blast 5 days ago.

I went to sleep thinking about the extremes in this country, where death often walks disguised beside you. Is a friend really a friend? The soft rolling hills came readily to my mind's eye, and were quickly darkened by an underlying feeling of impending pain for all who live in this country.

The day before, I had asked one of the news anchors with whom I worked, if it was hard to be a mom in all this violence. She told me, No, that Northern Ireland is statistically safer than most of America. I fell asleep thinking about what she had said.

I was jolted awake by a blast. The hotel shuddered, and the streets screamed with sirens. It was a man-made earthquake wrapped in centuries of anger and hate. It so rattled my psyche, that sleep eluded me.

When I went to work at Ulster a few hours later, the same news anchor who dismissed my questions of concern for raising a family smack in the middle of a centuries old war, told me, "You cannot imagine what I heard myself telling my daughter when the bombing started."

"What", I asked the reporter who looked incredibly tired and stressed..

"I said, don't be scared honey, it isn't thunder it is only the bombs. What is wrong with me? "

"The situation is wrong," I replied.

I told her about meeting Danny and she smiled knowingly. She wanted to know which tall tale I had heard. It was a much safer topic. Neither of us wanted to talk about the bombings.

Danny's stories were beautiful, but they meant even more than a few pounds and riches of the mind. I thought of what life had done to him, what had forced him to search out his "extraordinary" at eleven, and turn it into a business.

I wished he could just be a child.

If I had been my normal evening, answer email, check for text messages and Skyping my son, I would have missed Danny – and I would have missed the visceral link to Northern Ireland.

Be Open To The Unusual

An Extraordinary Day For Holding Hands

I dressed, undressed, re-dressed, changed shoes, looked in the mirror, sucked in my gut, and changed again. I wanted to be chic, serious, but not staid. I wanted to appear as if I just pulled a favorite outfit from my closet and put it on. In truth it had taken me hours of looking, trying, and buying to get close to what I wanted.

I was dressing for a meeting with a political candidate I was consulting. We were meeting at the candidate's ranch. Well, a sort of ranch. There were a few acres, a pool, and some guesthouses beside the main ranch house. Horses, but no cattle, just a little sanctuary from the frenzy of the smog filled Greek Capital, Athens.

I would again offer media advice, based on research, argue with those who "trusted their gut" more than the people with whom we had paid lots of money to poll, and plan our targeted message for the next political event.

We agreed on the goal, to get Miltiadis Evert elected to Greece's highest office – Prime Minister .

One of Mr. Evert's drivers picked me up, and like a typical Greek Driver, who believes the rules are for other drivers, paid no attention to the speed limit, or how many lanes were painted on the road. If all the lanes were full, he simply created an additional one. He cleverly drove on the median, or on the shoulder of the road;, whichever had the least amount of traffic. And did you know that in Greece, barely red lights are the same as green? Stop signs – less than a suggestion. I was generally on my cell phone when in the car – but not during this drive.

When we pulled off the main road and arrived at the ranch, I was thrilled that my wild carnival ride was over. The driver opened my door and I felt the sun burn the tops of my shoulders, but it was too hot for my jacket that I had thrown casually over my left shoulder. I also had my brief case in my left hand, trying to look like the briefcase weighed nothing, and I had everything under control.

Trying to avoid stumbling across the rocks to where the candidate and the rest of the group were waiting by the pool, I looked down. I did not want to bring a bruised chin, or scraped elbow to the negotiating table.

I felt it, before I saw it, before I realized what it was, before I slowed my heartbeat, steadied myself, and started breathing again. Someone with a large, rough hand had just taken mine in his. He held my hand rather tightly and did not let go. I willed myself not to look.

Did I say this hand was rough? Like an animal's feet that lived outdoors, rough? Oh, and this part – I know I have not told you this part. It was very hairy! I mean hairy. Gorilla hairy. I had to be polite, but I had to look…

Firmly grasping my hand was a full-grown chimpanzee!

Everyone burst out laughing, including me, and my new BFF. He swung my hand and tried to get me to run. He jumped up and down and swung my hand all the way to the pool.

When I sat down he tried to drink from my glass, when I said, "No that is my drink," he took my glass and ran, laughing and yowling as he went. Then he decided he wanted to spend the rest of the afternoon perched in my lap. It's sort of hard to be serious about politics when you have a laughing, belching monkey, turning your pages, and screeching when you give anyone else your attention.

Mr. Evert asked one of his ranch staff to put Mikro Mou (My Little One) back in his enormous cage. Mikro Mou protested his prison sentence by screaming and shaking the bars. He finally settled down, but I just knew he felt like I should spring him.

Miltiadis Evert passed just about a year ago. He did become President of the Conservative Party, but unfortunately never sat in the Prime Minister's Chair. Regardless, it takes an extraordinary man, with an extraordinary sense of humor, to choose an extraordinary animal to keep him company.

Doing EXTRAordinary Things Is a Choice

Many *regular* people do *extraordinary* things. Not to get attention, just to do the right thing. I believe that "acts of kindness" are never "random". People make choices early in life. It is part of their moral code. It is an integral center of who they are. The Dalai Lama XIV believes:

> *Our prime purpose in this life is to help others. If you can't help them, at least don't hurt them.*

From the outside, the good stuff people do, may seem like random acts of kindness. In reality, there is nothing random about *doing good*. It is a behavioral, life choice. When faced with an opportunity to do good – there is no question of, "Do I have time? Is it really important?" They just do it.

If you let them, people will surprise you with generosity and caring. One group of people's generosity simply knocked me out.

Straight From The Heart

I facilitated a teambuilding event, in upstate Vermont, soon after Irene huffed and puffed her way up the East Coast of the US.

Gaining strength, she loosed hell on Vermont, ripping up trees, turning century old covered bridges into piles of broken memories.

Irene spent her last breath blowing down houses, and washing out roads.

Furniture, rotted by the angry floods, sat in front yards of homes whose owners have no flood insurance.

No surprise. I mean, who would think of Vermont and hurricane in the same sentence?

At the conclusion of the event, which put 20 bikes into the hands of kids whose lives had been turned upside down, Chartis International looked into their upright world and wanted the kids to feel like there was a kind future, waiting for them. [1]

They passed the metaphorical hat for the kids of the community and came up with $2,200! It did not take forethought, a focus group, or strategic plan.

The question of "How can we brand this"? Or "How does this help us" was never uttered. It was anonymous kindness, and generosity, a response to a need. Dollars fell into a nondescript envelope, from the hands of people with extraordinary hearts and minds. They didn't get a tax break, no accolades at work, just a bunch of shy smiles from some kids who hadn't smiled at much lately. The company felt like it got more than it gave.

Countesy Independant Photograher

Choosing Kindness and Humor Over Ego
Disco Dancing With My Doctor

Nobody I know likes to talk about their internal plumbing. It was bad enough when we were kids and had to put up one or two fingers when asking to be excused for a trip to the restroom. All grown up, there is no code. You have to talk about stuff, explain stuff, and ask for help understanding stuff. All stuff that you do not want to talk about. Stuff that happening to all of us.

So how do you tell your doctor that you are concerned about well – what's happening or not happening in your gut? You go to my doctor who takes the discussion from embarrassing to entertaining.

Milk duds, like this? He asks pointing to a picture on what he calls his poop chart. Or more Baby Ruth, like this? What about Chocolate covered raisins?

Well, you get the picture. My extraordinary doctor doesn't take himself too seriously. It is clear that he gets the humiliation and embarrassment that accompanies a trip to see him, a gastroenterologist. He chose early on to let his sunny personality do the talking, explaining and showing. Who else would turn a poop chart into a sweet explanation? (By the way, he gave me a laminated copy I can use as a guide, and bookmark if I am really desperate.)

He even remembers who you are if he meets you in a hallway – and it's not exactly your face he gets to know. But candy charts are only the beginning. He lets his entire good-natured personality shine on everyone who has the pleasure of working with him or is a patient.

Fridays are his surgery days, and he turns them into play dates for all. He loves disco music, and everyone loves him.

> *How do you like it? How do you like it?*
> *More, more, more.*

Tapping my toes to the rock of the 80's under the lights of a disco ball, I wanted to bust a Donna Summer's move, but I was a little tied up, with an IV in my arm, dressed in a "one tie in the back" outfit not fit for disco.

No John Travolta, or Bee Gees, but there were several people wearing costumes with gloves, and mouthing the words to disco songs.

One of them put a nice warm blanket over me and someone else let me know that my disco doctor, the star of the show, would be in shortly. That made me smile. Of course there were drugs. I had a needle in my arm. I was pretty relaxed. It was not my first time dancing to disco on my creative, caring, doctor's Disco Friday.

One of the techs asked if I liked the Bee Gees or Travolta.

No brainer. I asked for Disco Queen Donna. This procedure just got a whole lot less humiliating.

I was having a bit of my recalcitrant stomach-ulcer snatched for a little more exploration, and the lower pipelines checked out as well, all to the tunes of Saturday Night Fever, under the glitter of a disco ball. Compliments of my doctor.

I believe most surgeons have traded their sense of humor for a God complex. Not my doctor. His whole demeanor is one of caring, making his patients smile, and banishing fear.

He put me back together after I managed to throw up a few buckets of blood in front of the lunch crowd at an IHop. (I am certain that I am now on the international IHop "no serve list"). I got treated to a racy ride, on a gurney, in the back of a howling ambulance, with a couple of "very serious" EMTs. My doctor met me at the hospital.

A few units of blood, and a little surgery later, my doctor showed me where the vampire took a bite out of my stomach. He described it as a real monster, and assured me, he had zapped it good. In no time I was back on my feet, with pictures for Facebook. Kidding. But back to Disco Friday...

My doctor takes his work seriously, but not himself. Finding himself without a note pad, after his every 8 months check of my internal parts, he writes my pharmacy's phone number on his surgical scrubs, and says, "We can just send my pants to the pharmacy." We all laugh.

He added that, on a day like this, it was okay to stink up the place. In fact the stinkier it got – the better I would feel.

My husband assured him the process was well under way. I turned sixty shades of red, thanked him for the Disco Session and we were on our way home.

CONNIE TIMPSON

Part Two
Explore The Extraordinary

Your EXTRAordinary
Is Like No Other

Your EXTRAordinary — is unique. No one else thinks feels, acts, or responds to situations or people, just like you do.

I met these two cuties on a beach.

Twins, but Mom told me — *they are nothing alike.* One is outgoing and adventurous, the other is timid and shy.

Psychologists have long used sets of twins to determine the effects of nurture vs. nature - same household, same parents, and experiences. Similar outcome? Not as often as you might think.

They often turn out quite different, in height, looks, and personalities – one independent, a maker of friends, the other – not so much. Take our twin nieces for example:

One *believes* she is a princess. The other vacillates between super hero, athlete, and rock star.

A little trip to the Florida Keys produced this anecdote:
Approaching the escalator, Princess Jackie, let's go of the handle of her bag and says, "Dad, would you get that" not a question, a statement of entitlement.

(She really is the best of all princesses – sweet, caring, affable, adorable, but has high expectations.)

On the other hand, Stephanie's eyes hold the glow of "I can do anything!" Need a sitter for your alligator? Call Steph.

She is not big on being a princess but does don a sequin studded tulle skirt, leggings and pink cowboy boots when she is in her Rock Star mode.

Certainly Identical twins are identical. Right?

Not necessarily. A new study by Geneticist Carl Bruder of the University of Alabama found that in some cases, one twin's DNA differed from the other twins at various points on their genomes.

So looking alike, dressing alike, even identical gestures, *may not be exactly identical.*

Many people are extraordinary, and do extraordinary things. We simply have to look - to see their individual, extraordinary, acts. Many of them just make life a little easier, and a whole lot more interesting.

> *Clearly –*
> *Identical isn't always*
> *Identical!*

Boot the Labels Out of Your Subconscious

We get stuck with labels as soon as the stork touches down.

The same babies *we* labeled deftly pick up the labeling tool as soon as they learn to speak. *Bad dog. Icky kid. Mean teacher.* And the labeling grows, both in intent and number of categories - *stutterer, carrot top, nerdster, brainiac, wimp.*

This prejudicial labeling continues throughout life, perpetuated by all of us – the labelers. Any of these labels sound familiar - *crazy boss, best professor, deadbeat dad, or super mom?*

We categorize people, without thinking. We metaphorically plant stickers on their foreheads, chests, wherever the label is easy to read.

Kind
Unhappy
Smart
Successful
Failure

Many politicians are master labelers. Sometimes, a bit like bullies in grade school, acting out between classes. Stick on as many negative stickers as possible before the bell rings, yell, "You're it!" and run.

We form expectations that reach to that little reptilian part of our brain, to our "way back" ancestors. There is but one question.

Will it eat me?!?

If the other being looks different, we are far more likely to be hesitant, to trust less. If the other being looks, and acts like us, he is like us right? Not exactly. He may even dress like us. None of us, however, are *exactly* the same.

Put down the label gun. In fact, lock it in a lock box. Rip off the labels that you have already stuck on people, and look beneath them. We may think we know someone, and find out that our labeler misfired, or was superficial at best. No one should be labeled, or categorized.

I had interviewed County Commissioner, George Shiozawa, many times. He was a serious, studied, well-informed, and fair, public servant. I had labeled him as a consummate professional, never addressing his real person, never looking under the label I had given him, until one American Anniversary that prompted me to call on him for a reason other than county business.

It was the anniversary of the day Japan shocked the world by attacking Pearl Harbor. I wanted a different take, a time seen through the eyes of a Japanese-American child, the day the unthinkable happened.

What I got, was a look into the heart of one of the most extraordinary people I have ever met.

Extraordinary Forgiveness Injustice and Mistrust

We set up the equipment, babbled about county business, and my video partner signaled that we were ready. I asked Commissioner Shiozowa to tell me about the day his family heard the news of Pearl Harbor, and what that meant to him.

"I was just ten years old, and as we walked home from church an Army truck pulled up in front of our house. It frightened me and I hid behind my mother and wrapped myself in her skirt.

Soldiers demanded to see what we had worked so hard to gain - our citizenship papers. They searched our house, taking family documents and photos, all the kitchen knives and my pearl-handled pocketknife, a treasured gift from my uncle. We hoped it was over.

We were wrong.

Two days later, the soldiers returned. They loaded us like cattle into the backs of trucks and took us away. I was so frightened I did not speak for days. Finally we reached the Idaho desert. We were cold, afraid, and our hearts bruised by the country we loved.

Soldiers with hard faces, penned us, like cattle, behind barbed wire. The world was closed to us, just because we looked different. America is made up of immigrants.

As prisoners in our own country, we lived in an internment camp, while our brothers fought the Japanese. The cold of winter made us huddle, and the sand storms of summer made us wake with grit in our eyes. The walls were filled with nothing but hope. The cracks in the walls allowed the raw, desert elements to torture us.

(Over 120,000 Japanese-Americans were interned during World War II)

YOU ARE EXTRAORDINARY!

His last sentence prompted one big tear to run down his regal, stoic face, and its image lodge in my heart. I turned to signal my video partner to stop the camera, and saw that this, work-out-at-the-gym, I can do anything guy, had tears in his eyes.

The narrow label of "Commissioner" had been ripped off. I would never again see Commissioner George Shiozowa in the same way. He had allowed us to gain entrance into his inner self, that place that tells nothing but truth.

Until that day, I had no idea how EXTRAordinary this man was, nor how ignorant I had been growing up in rural Idaho. I went to school with Nakiyama kids, Fugimoto kids, and Shiozowa's. I was ashamed that I never questioned why until I was in High School. Only then, did I begin researching what had happened. Now, all the books I had sought out meant nothing compared to the man who sat in front of me.

Commissioner Shiozowa used this unbearably painful chapter in his life, to tell his own story, to reveal the shameful history of America.

Defying Every Label
Trading Labels For Gold

Native American, Lakota Kid, Orphan, the Indian kid who won't drink, the Oglala Lakota who can run.

Billy Mills accepted none of the labels life tried to stick on him.

Born an impoverished Native American, losing his mother at age seven, and his father at 12, Mills began running to overcome his pain and anguish. The hills, the smell of sagebrush, and the changing colors of the land as the sun shifted, became his sanctuary. He defied every label, winning a scholarship to university, where he shined.

He did not stop there. This Lakota kid would show the world what EXTRAORDINARY looks like. In 1964, just back from service in Korea, this Native American stunned the world in the Tokyo Olympics.

During the last lap of the race, Mills was elbowed by the Tunisian runner, all but fell, regained his footing, and like the wind, passed the Australian who was the odds on favorite and broke the tape.

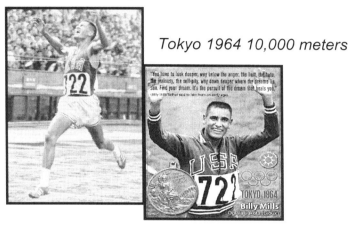

Tokyo 1964 10,000 meters

Even American sportscasters were shocked. He was not on their list of "Top Contenders." In fact they had to look at a roster to find his name, and he was running in borrowed shoes. Only real contenders got new ones.

Now screaming like little girls meeting Mylie Cyrus, they watched Mills break the tape, setting a new world record for the 10,000 meter. He now wore the title of Gold Medal Winner.

What Billy Mills did that day is extraordinary, but who he is, is the most extraordinary.

He could have gone on to do television commercials; appeared on cereal boxes, or just about anything he wanted under the banner of his new found fame. Rather than choosing ego, or the ability to become very, very rich, he chose to become even more extraordinary.

I interviewed Mills, a few years back when he spoke at a Native American Youth Conference. He is the "real deal." What he does, and says, is straight from his heart, and you cannot help but feel it enter yours.

He devotes his life to saving the physical and spiritual lives of America's young Native Americans.

Among a group of young adults, where drinking is not usually a question, but an answer to an often miserable existence, he persuades young Native Americans to look at their "inner person" to have the strength to say no to peer pressure.

He helps them develop a better sense of self. To embrace the concept that, "They can do anything they want to do, that they can become real contenders." They can be extraordinary.

The obvious question, how did Billy Mills do what no one imagined he could do, "I visualized. My grandfather taught me how. I saw myself running. I saw myself winning. I would not let doubt come into my head. During that last lap, I heard nothing but the beating of my heart."

His eyes shine with the clarity of passion, self-belief, and the potential in others. His life's work is to persuade and inspire.

Success, Mills told me, comes from setting goals, never losing sight of what can be, and who you are.

He is truly one of the most inspiring people I have ever met.

There is a movie based on his life, "Running Brave". Robby Benson stars in it. It is good, but it is Hollywood.

Mills is the real EXTRAordinary!

First Encounter Snapshots

Managing Our "Thin Slices"

We all do it – take psychological snapshots at high-shutter speeds when gauging a new situation.

The term "Thin Slices" was first coined in 1992 by Nalini Ambady and Robert Rosenthal and mainstreamed by Malcolm Gladwell in his 2005 bestseller "Blink", thinking that happens in the blink of an eye.

Our perception of others comes from what biases or impressions we have been imprinted with, until something changes our knowledge or impressions. Psychologists like Ambady, have proven, in study after study, that most of those first snapshots are accurate – but not always.

Some Snapshots Distort and Need Immediate Editing

Stepping out of a women's shelter on Chicago's South side, I felt good about my day. I was tired, but pleased. I had cooked, helped kids with homework, and hopefully left a little role modeling behind.

I pulled the collar of my coat up tight against the freezing cold and snow, and looked around. In the failing light I saw my little, red, two-seater Honda. It was surrounded by a bunch of teenagers in droopy pants, and knit caps.

Automatically, I took a step back, my heart in my throat. This is not the "kind" or "rich "side of town. The streets are more than mean. They are often deadly.

Only when I grasped the door handle did I remember that it automatically locks when it closes. I rang the bell, trying to look nonchalant, as fear dripped down my chest. No one answered.

One of the boys walked towards me and I panicked, my back now tight against the door. He held his hand up and said, "Mam, Mam, please don't worry. We are making sure your ride is okay. My Mom and two little ones are inside the shelter. Don't want nothin to happen to your car."

My heart flooded with warm relief; and was immediately cooled by shame. This group of young men were too old for the shelter, but too young to be on their own. All of my, "it is a dangerous neighborhood," thoughts had pushed out any of my "these people are just like me" beliefs. I was embarrassed. Ashamed. And I was immediately apologetic.

The shelter's door did not re-open that night, and I did not knock again. I did not need to. The young men saw to it that I got safely to my car. I thanked them, gave them the only $20 I had, (which they tried to refuse) and drove back to Hyde Park – the "kind" and "rich" part of Chicago.

I was still shaking when I entered my office on the University of Chicago Campus. My assessment of the situation, my snapshot, needed to be edited.

I had felt vulnerable, threatened, and what I now felt was thankful and ashamed. These young men, living in a hostile world, were EXTRAordinary.

I went back to the shelter several times after that. The boys, always waiting, just to make sure I got safely to my car. As one boy told me, "Ya just can't be too careful." His dark, kind eyes, now my snapshot. My thin slice.

Her Whole World Had Been Photo-Shopped

Through government manipulation Maria saw something very different from reality. Plutocrats had photo-shopped the world, to show her a carefully constructed, photo collage of a powerful country. They had more "stuff" than any other nation.

More wealth, higher education, advanced technology, more brilliant scientists, the most well written literature in the world, simply more power, prestige and progress. That is the altered picture of the Soviet Union that Maria saw, and believed, while growing up.

Then glasnost, and perestroika, involuntarily hit the "undo" button on the photo-editing program, and Maria's collage began to dissolve, many of the pictures at the same time.

Maria was shocked at the now, gray, distorted, images. She found out that she did not live in the most powerful country in the world. The Soviet Union was not rich, not advanced, not a leader in the world of literature.

We met, while I was training journalists to navigate their way through the landscape of "news that is balanced, with no government control." (In theory.)

Maria's New Reality

I handed Maria a copy of Vogue I had promised to bring to Russia. The glossy pages took her captive.

"How do you know the images are real?" And news magazines, aren't they censored? "No, not really."

Her disappointment and disillusionment of her Soviet world was palpable, her understanding of journalism was shattered.

We sipped coffee in a stunning room within the swank Metropol Hotel. This was the same hotel that my friend, Maria Ivanian, had been thrown out of when the Soviet Union was still under its "Red" lock down. She told me that during those years, it was illegal for her to be there because she was of the Proletariat, and the Metropol was a Communist Party place. She could have been sent to prison.

Her freedom to have a cup of coffee with an American at the Metropol - made the coffee very sweet.

YOU ARE EXTRAORDINARY!

Now she is a consultant to the Duma, you might say a lobbyist for Non Governmental Agencies. Yes, capitalism has reached the former communist country, and she is part of it. We went into the Duma, and sat for a while in her office to talk about her projects.

All at once she leaned back in her chair, stretched and basked in the sunshine, allowing the promise of tomorrow envelop her. Money was not easy, but smiling was.

She wanted to show me the artistry of her country. It had somehow survived, during the time that the KGB could be just a knock away.

We did not go to a museum, nor to the Pushkin, we went to the underground subway. Nothing Maria said prepared me for what I saw.

The décor came at the time of artistic opulence. It was the 30's and Art Deco was the Russian rage.

The marble walls arch gracefully to domed passageways, giving way to the platforms, lighted by stunning Art Deco wall lamps.

Platform to platform, you must ride the escalators. The passageway is so steep that when you step on an up escalator and look across to the escalator moving people down, it looks as if they are lying on their backs. To the people moving further into the belly of the city, we look like we are tipping over, falling on our faces.

The deco lamps, illuminate Russian faces, giving their skin a translucent glow, as the flying stairs carry them from here to there, like a Salvador Dali painting come to life.

Reading my awe-struck expression, Maria tells me it is the best way to get through the belly of the sprawling city of Moscow. I would take it every day if I could!

Maria's favorite subway station instantly became my favorite. It is like a wing of the Louvre, or a hall of a 30's Pushkin.

It is called the War Station. Bronze, life-sized statues hold up the corners of each entry to a different passageway.

There were old men, cast in bronze as they lived and served in Russian history, beside young soldiers of war. They seemed to look back at us, with eyes that had seen too much.

Honoring the equality of women under communist rule, there were bronze statues of women with children, pregnant women, old women, women of science, women wearing the traditional babushka; planting fields, sweeping; all with guns, all with the gleam of Russian pride in their eyes.

Every face, hand, each strand of hair, was meticulously drawn, and cast. No detail, or emotion was too small. They stood like giants, with the pride of their creators, vanguards of artistic times.

This, Maria tells me, is Russia. Our bones, our people. This is why we will survive."

Survivors they are. In cold that burned my lungs like liquid nitrogen, we went to an outdoor market and waited in line, after line, after line, for orange juice, biscuits, coffee and cheese.

I had long given up on my feet, dragging them around like blocks of solid ice.

All the while we waited and waited, Maria remarked that shopping was so much better now that Russia was open to the world. They had more choices, and the lines were shorter.

I was there ten years earlier. I too remember the lines, and the empty shelves once you inched your way to the front, no longer feeling your feet, all the while, thinking that starving may be better than freezing.

YOU ARE EXTRAORDINARY!

She asked me about shopping in America. The possibility of a photograph thankfully did not give me time to reply. Maria pointed out a man, obviously of Indian descent, pushing his child in a stroller. I pantomimed that I would like to photograph his child. He smiled, and nodded.
Maria tells me that many rich Indians come to Moscow to study.

The face of Russia is as complex as that of America, and that alone assures Maria that Russia will survive.

Packages in tow, we start off for the flat that Maria shares with her parents. Maria's parents are doctors. She tells me that her family has a nicer apartment than most, and they do not have to share their flat with anyone else.

While Maria unlocks four sets of locks on the door, she explains that the woman sitting in the hallway was asking who I am. Maria whispers that the woman reports strangers who come into the building. I wince a little, and try to think of her as a doorkeeper, and not a leftover snitch from communist days. She answers my questioning eyes that look back at the locks.

"Moscow is not so safe, any more."

I remembered, years before that if someone was following you, it was a member of Intourist, or the KGB, not a mugger. Once inside, we make coffee, eat Russian cakes; and Maria shares her dreams, of becoming more powerful as a consultant/lobbyist in the Duma.

She tells me that women prospered in the communist era, that they were totally equal to men when it came to education, even jobs. The biggest problem, she told me, was the classist system that ruled a supposedly "class-free" society.

It hurt everyone, but the elite and corrupt. Now, she says the corrupt run everything, but she wants to change that, to make Russia a place where all prosper.

Maria has the future in her eye, and pride in her step. She is part of the new Russia, a guide for others, a woman who will not Photoshop history. She assures me that this new openness "Glasnost" will ensure an accurate photograph of her country and her life.

Explore *Your EXTRAordinary*

Let your extraordinary out. Explore your gifts, and share them with us. Don't be shy.

You can uncover your own inner extraordinary. Your *"no one has anything like it"* wealth. One of the first steps is to recognize "extraordinary" in others.

Open your heart and mind to the possibilities, and be willing to take some risks to get the rewards.

I took a risk to live and work in Pakistan. What I got back was a lifetime of EXTRAordinary. I went to teach Afghan women journalists how to create documentaries, so that they could document their own situation. I met many extraordinary people, who took extraordinary risks to keep their dreams alive.

Many of them lost everything, first to the communists, then to the Taliban. Stripped of their physical possessions, holding on only by sheer will and courage, they survived by embracing their beliefs and inner strength, their individual *Extraordinary* lodged in the center of their hearts.

Colors of Courage

Women on campus started a revolt by displaying a green chador, a simple headscarf, on the end of a gun. Green is the color of Islam and the women wanted to be included in society, not silenced by purdah. (Separation of men and women)

"We wanted them to know we were ready to fight for what we believed in." Parwin tells me.

None of the teachers, or students, imagined how one green scarf would rock their lives. Parwin says, "Before anyone knew what was happening there were shots, screaming students, then students who lie still, filling the grass with the last moments of their lives."

Many died right there. Others were taken away, treated at hospitals, where more students died. Some were arrested, tortured, and made to tell that Parwin was one of the leaders.

She knew they would tell. They would have to. No one could stand the pain. She knew the men with guns would come for her.

"Terrified and pregnant, I was dragged from my home into the blackened night, by soldiers from the Kabul regime. I would only tell them that I belonged to the party of Islam. That enraged them. They told me my husband had betrayed me. I knew that was not true. Our life was built on respect for each other and honesty. He was not a man who believed that women were less than men.

These men pushed me, beat me, pulled hunks of hair from my head. Finally they hooked electric wires to my toes and hands. It sent me mad, biting my lips and tongue. Blood ran into my ears, until I passed out.

I remember nothing else until I awoke to my bloody dead child lying like ice across my stomach, the umbilical cord still attached. I fell unconscious."

Her life in shambles, her husband missing, Parwin knew that to survive, to protect her two remaining children, she must leave. After nearly freezing to death crossing the Khyber Pass, Parwin made it to Islamabad, and into the arms of what she believed was safety.

As soon as her feet were on solid soil, she helped start a school. Education for women, she told me, could not be lost. She gets hate calls in the night. The caller threatens that if she continues to teach, she will die. She won't quit. She says if she were to stay at home she would feel small, dead inside, that education is that important.

She is not afraid of dying she says, one day it will happen and she cannot change destiny. "I have seen all there is to see. I am sorrow proof. If I die in the way of Islam, it will be good."

When in public with these women, I dressed in the Pakistani, Shalwar Kameez, and wrapped a scarf, a chador, around my hair. It was a simple sign of respect. More importantly, If I dressed as an American, I put all of these women at risk of being attacked by Islamic fundamentalists. The threat is real.

In Peshawar, the Mullahs, with newfound power, trolled the markets looking for women whom, they judged were not properly covered. In a Burka, you were safe, that is unless you stepped on the front of it and fell, as I saw more than once. If a chador (headscarf) slipped out of place while carrying packages, some of the Mullahs may throw acid in the woman's face, scarring her for life. I met women like that, disfigured, just because while burdened with food for their family, a scarf shifted showing an inch of hair.

Few of us have faced such difficulty and fear. Few of us are pushed to find our "inner extraordinary" in this way. Afghanistan, and the territories of Pakistan have not changed. Abuse and subjugation of women has become the norm.

I had to leave Pakistan long before I was ready, before I had done all I could, and wanted to do. I had fallen in love with the plight of these women. As the Taliban's power grew, so did their distrust and dislike of America. I was threatened.

The now fundamentalist brothers and fathers, of the very girls I taught came to the school armed with Russian Kalashnikovs, and threats to make their point. They spray painted "Death to the American" on our building. I happened to be in Peshawar for meetings. I could not believe what I was seeing and hearing on my return.

The Canadian and American embassies that brought me to Pakistan now thought it best that I leave. They felt responsible for my safety. I barely got to say good-bye to my Afghan students before I was put on a plane.

Coming home was a hard transition for me. This time, I felt small, embarrassed at the wealth of safety with which I could walk American streets, go the supermarket without my husband or brother, or dress in a mini skirt, if I had wanted to. Few of us have had to fight for our lives and beliefs to be educated.

All of these women took risks to learn. Many fought just to stay alive. I hold these precious women in my heart, a beat away from the surface. All of them were extraordinary.

What Makes *You* Extraordinary?
(Yes you are – explore it.)

What makes you special, different, extraordinary? What makes you feel like you have earned passage among others? Yes, you have it. You have earned it, developed it, and perfected much of your extraordinariness.

Ask yourself what makes you feel joy, what makes your heart swell with pride, what gives you courage?

Ease up on the self-control, and let *your extraordinary* direct you.

Connect to your inner self, and let your best self, bubble to the surface.

What makes your heart pound, or just feel full of good stuff? Not what you work at. That is not "who you are". Do not let yourself be defined by what you do to make a living.

Let Your EXTRAordinary Run Free!

Run after what you really want.

Let yourself *see and feel* – tap into the visceral center of your body. Feel what your center wants and needs. There are no limits, no expectations, no judgments allowed. (No, this is not a pitch for yoga. It is a get in touch with what you want in life pitch.) Put the mat away.

What are your passions, the ones you have pushed to the back of your emotional closet?

Slide the door open, and try them on – no restrictions. You can make anything fit. Some of it, will however, fit you better than other things.

Find what makes you feel the best, and wear it like winged armor.

- ✓ Music
- ✓ Animals
- ✓ Painting
- ✓ Writing
- ✓ Environment
- ✓ Children

It is never too late to discover and embrace the kind of person life has pushed you to conform to.

It takes courage to take risks. There is no guaranteed outcome, except that your self-esteem will grow, just because you questioned, tried, and took a risk – on *YOU*.

Most of us have no idea that we have mountain-high strength, or courage. It often takes an event, a situation, something that pushes us out of our comfort zone. Let it.

One, extraordinary woman, had no idea she had such determination, such courage, such self-less love for others, until something pushed her to take a microscopic look at everything she knew. She discovered her strength, when her own body attacked her, and she wanted to share her life lessons with others.

Extraordinary Courage, Caring, and Determination

My phone rang as I stepped into the newsroom. I figured it would be someone complaining about something we had just aired. It wasn't. The following story is as close to the exact words as I can remember.

Connie, my name is Ann Huller. I have a curious offer to make.

I'm listening.

I would like you to document my story of teaching children how to let go, say goodbye to someone, or some thing, they love.

I waited for more, thinking, "It is sort of an interesting idea."

I think it would work well in your "For Kids Sake" segment. You see, I am a kindergarten teacher, and I want to teach my children how to let go, how to say goodbye. I do not have much time. There was no question what she meant.

I was stunned into silence for a split second and then asked if we could meet the next day. It was "bond at first sight." We began an adventure. Her story would take about six months to tell. There could be no follow up. It was what it was.

Ann Huller was dying of lung cancer.

No, no reprieves. She tried to deny that something was amiss with her health for a long time. It was too long. Doctors tried everything. The drug cocktails made her very ill. Radiation made her sicker than the cocktails. She stopped taking any kind of treatment. She told me that any treatment that would hopefully extend her life – made her want to summon her mother to show her the door to the afterlife immediately.

There was another reason Ann declined treatment. She wanted to be totally in control as she taught the little ones in her classes how to say goodbye to people they love.

She needed all of herself to make sure she got her message right. The parents gave their okay to Ann's request. Her last lesson would be difficult. She did not want to simply disappear from the lived of these precious children.

Her class of 20 adorable children - adored her. She was about to impart the most important lesson life has to teach us.

We started shooting among what seemed to be, a million, 5 year old inquisitors. Why were we here? Were we taking pictures for their parents? Did we know their teacher? How does the camera work? What do you write in that notebook?

They got used to us, like the chalkboard in the classroom. We taped this process, the children, and this extraordinary woman who would teach them first hand, that life is to be experienced, savored, and those whom you meet along the way, loved, and held close.

Ann used the book, "The Fall of Freddy The Leaf" to begin life's most difficult conversation – letting go of people we love. Freddy is born a light-green shoot, and grows into a supple-green leaf.

He spreads his fingertips, reaching to the sun, to absorb copper and gold colors from his big round friend in the sky. Absorbing the heat, Freddy grows old, becomes weightless, finally falling to the ground where he crackles apart and becomes part of the earth. Starting the life cycle over.

We shot a lot of tape over the next few months, and I cried a lot of tears. So did the tough-guy photographer who helped me tell Ann's story. I was proud to put something on television that was so honest.

I saw Ann regularly, and each time she was thinner than the last. She began having more bad days than good, and doctors banned everyone but her husband and two grown children. I missed her.

As I went to the studio to anchor the news one night, I was handed a phone message from Ann's son.

Ann's mother had come for her.

You can never be really ready to lose someone whom has made your life a better one to live.

I had to tell all those who had come to admire this extraordinary woman, that like Freddy, Ann's season had ended. My voice cracked and my eyes glistened as I told viewers we had lost Ann. Those who followed her story, and came to love Ann as I did, called and left messages. They thanked me for sharing this woman's story.

They did not expect me to return their calls. We were in this together.

The lessons - This incredible woman inspired many of us to do more, do better, accept the life cycle, and say goodbye. Ann had given me a most rare gift - a life lesson wrapped in caring and inspiration. She did it by courageously sharing her story with a vast audience. On days when I think life is a little difficult I remember Ann's lessons, her smile, mostly her courage.

Most of us have no idea that we have mountain-high strength, or courage. It often takes an event, a situation, something that pushes us out of our comfort zone. Let it.

This extraordinary woman had no idea she had such determination, such courage and such selfless love for others. She did.

As American guru, Leo F. Busgaglia said, "Too often we underestimate the power of a touch, a smile, a kind word, a listening ear, an honest compliment, or the smallest act of caring, all of which have the potential to turn a life around." [2]

---

[2] Leo Busgaglia – "Love" 1972

The Truly Extraordinary Walk Among Us

There are heroes among us. Many. We know some of them personally. Others – we know because they belong to everyone. They are public - the Gabbie Giffords, the Sully Sullenbergers, the Randy Pausch's, New York's 9/11 rescue teams, the extraordinary heroes who worked their way into Pakistan, like smoke in the night, and brought down Osama. Just Navy Seals doing their job.

I see extraordinary heroes in every airport I ever walk through, American soldiers going to, or coming from, a war zone. They are dressed in camouflage, a little shy when some of us reach out to say, "Be safe, and thank you".

I try not to listen or look. But their nervous smiles are a magnet to the heart. The ones with shine in their eyes are on their way to the Iraq desert, or the killing streets and mountain hideouts of Afghanistan.

Those, excited to be home, look at their little brothers from hooded eyes. They were there, seen it all too closely, and felt the fires of hell lapping at their heels.

The shiny-eyed boys and girls will exchange places with the lucky ones who raced to one of the, few remaining, banks of phones to tell family and friends that they have one more connection and they will be home. As I looked on, unable to divert my eyes, the desert virgins shook hands with their experienced brothers believing they too will come home.

Alive. Whole. Borrowed by their country. Not spent.

I hear one of the "seen too much guys" tell a skinny soldier in brand new desert camo, "It's no picnic over there, but it'll be okay."

A boy, with hair too short to feel the teeth of a comb, pops his gum and shakes hands with another soon to be, sandstorm brother. He looks so young. I am surprised he is old enough to sign the papers that sent him to boot camp and now require him to put on a soldier's uniform and board a plane.

As I watch, he raises a hand to adjust the backpack that pulls him to one side and a gleam of gold on a finger catches my eye. It is bright. New. A promise to come home.

Tubbs is written across his right-chest pocket and U.S. Army on the left. I silently pray that Tubbs does come home, that he will be able to throw a football with the kids I imagine he does not yet have.

You do not, however, have to become a soldier, or a pilot safely landing a troubled airplane on the Hudson River to be extraordinary. It takes a little courage and strength. It takes an internal look, and commitment to your own *Extraordinary.*

A Mysterious Box
And An Extraordinary Dad

I had my hand stuck inside the cat carrier, trying to assure Charlie, who is a cat with the personality of political satirist John Stewart, that the barking, sniffing, growling dogs would not hurt him.

I hoped.

If he could, Charlie would tell them sarcastically that he believed in a separation of church and state, and more importantly Cats and Dogs! Now step off, and shut up!

The door to the veterinary clinic opened and in walked a man carrying a box, with three small children clinging to it. They sat down next to me and they all wanted to pet Charlie. He can't be trusted not to take a nibble when he's stressed, so I suggested they just look through the screen.

Trying to diffuse their attention from Charlie, I asked what they had in their box. They convinced their Dad that I had to see their "broken friend."

I was a little nervous. I mean, what could be in a big cardboard box with the lid closed making sort of slithering, scratching noises?

Trying to be a grown-up who does not freak out, I peaked through the tucked together flaps. It was a giant turtle! Wow!

"What is wrong with him?" I asked Dad. He opened the box to show me that someone or something had broken his shell. This little family of turtle savers had driven for two hours to get to the only veterinarian who thought he could help.

The nurse told me I could take Charlie back, but the big sad eyes of three small children prompted me to offer my slot to the dad who had rescued a turtle, so that his little ones would smile again.

Ten minutes later Dad and the kids walked back into the waiting room, tears turned to smiles. The little girl with pigtails ran to me and grabbed my hand.

"Look, look. He's glued back together!" Indeed he was. Who knew you could superglue a broken turtle and mend some little hearts at the same time?

This dad was definitely a hero. The turtle, now dubbed "Sammy" was headed back to Georgia. The little girl told me, so he could find his family. Dad just smiled.

Extraordinary Lessons From Behind a Fallen Facade

A little over ten years ago, I worked with the evolving Slovakia, to develop news as a business at small television stations. The idea that news should be balanced was a *foreign* concept to this country that had every word, checked, rechecked, approved, or purely dictated by the communists. They were small, but hungry. They were eager to learn about American style news.

Not much equipment, but plenty of intellect and desire to bring the world into what was their "closed society."

First I needed to understand their culture. They shared stories of life under Moscow's thumb, putting a human face on this little known history.

At the heart of one extraordinary man's story was one of my favorite authors, Milan Kundera, the author of The Unbearable Lightness of Being. Stanislov Prokes would learn American style television from me, and I would learn more about determination and courage from Stanislov Prokes, of Sen TV than I could have ever imagined.

Risk Everything To Let The Soul Live

We were afraid. So afraid. But I had to take the risk. I had to continue to be some of what I was before our freedom was taken. We passed Kundera's book of stories "Laughable Loves" from hand-to-hand. We hid it inside the communist newspaper, at the bottom of a basket of bread, or inside a pile of laundry. We carefully tucked the book inside anything that looked innocent. We had to avoid being checked by police.

We were careful. We had to be very careful. It only took one mistake to end up in Siberia. Sometimes, it did not even take one mistake. We worked only after covering the windows. A tiny glow from a candle allowed us to read Kundera's words.

Daylight rarely fell on these treasured pages. If it did, we immediately hid the book, from the government, that seemed to have Xray vision.

At night, whoever had the book, would pull it from hiding and re-type Kundera's words, the next few pages for us to read. We would roll as much carbon paper into the typewriter as we could, and type as quickly as possible.

We read it the way we copied it, a few pages at a time. That way only one person could be caught with the whole book. Yes, it was illegal, what we did. We could have gone to prison.

Owning books was dangerous, a threat against the state. But reading Kundera's stories of Czech life before the invasion was worth the risk. They could take my freedom, but not my love of words.

I was an intellectual, so the government pulled me out of the University and sent me to work in a chlorine factory. The smell, the disgusting smell of chlorine, its poison, was always stuck in my nose.

I craved the smell of books. I missed handling books, touching them, reading, and exchanging ideas with colleagues. Holding Kundera's words in my hand was like holding a sacred scripture.

Kundera fled to France when Russia rolled its tanks into Czechoslovakia. Bookstores and libraries were stripped of his words.

Kundera's personal story and struggle, made sharing the book, "Laughable Loves" a sacred mission for those behind the wall. They fought to read every word with ink on their fingers that if discovered, could cost them everything.

Saying goodbye, and readying to board a plane in Bratislava, my host Stan Sr. handed me a small package.

"Open it," he urged.

The book, that Stan risked his freedom to share with fellow intellectual risk takers, lay in my hands.

I tried to decline this precious gift, handing it back to him. He pocketed his hands, telling me that the book was now mine because I understood his people and appreciated the hands that shared and protected this book. I held it, fighting back tears, but lost.

Stan and his cohorts in "spreading illegal literature" risked everything to protect and share Kundera's stories.

It is now mine to protect and treasure.

When I touch the tiny, battered book, I sometimes think I can feel the spirit of determination and some of the courage it took to protect it. It humbles me, greatly.

Its 98 pages seem to give off a mystical feeling of defiance, and hope for the future. More importantly I feel Stan's extraordinariness, his courage and determination to share what he held sacred.

"Laughable Loves" sits on my desk where I can see it nearly every day. It humbles me, inspires me, and reminds me of an extraordinary person who can now read anything he wants.

The American Dream
One Frightening Mile At A Time

He is the pied piper of kids. They gravitate to him. Little kids, big kids, they all want to be next to Jose. This quiet man guides, loves, stands up for his beliefs, and constantly smiles. Not a grin, a gentle, kind, and wise smile. Perhaps most important, is the way *he listens.* Really listens, does not judge, just listens, offering advice only if asked for it.

This relatively young man, whose "old" spirit shines in his eyes, is living proof that the American Dream is alive. That extraordinary people exist, and can become a beautiful stitch in the fabric of America.

Jose's "Coming to America" story began when he and his two brothers were small enough to lie like possums on the floorboards of a car, his mother and uncle hidden under blankets in the trunk. Every peso they had, every dream, and breath they drew, was in the hands of a Coyote, a smuggler of desperate human beings.

For three days there were no rest stops, no roadside diners, only an anonymous, dingy, room for a few hours in the middle of the night. The family stepped soundlessly; listening for a sound, a word, that they had been discovered and sent back to a life they could not bare.

Finally inside the United States, the ordeal was not yet over. The family lived on the edge of society, not quite fitting in, never feeling quite safe.

Jose's determined Mom made tough decisions. Education outweighed the fear of deportation, so the kids went to school, easily picking up English, while she worked a minimum wage job.

Maria is a good person, people liked her, gave her a kind nod when they knew that ICS would show up at work. That meant she would stay at home, missing a day of wages that the family sorely needed. She so wanted to fit in, wanted her kids to fit in; that struggling became her normal state of mind.

Jose recalls his kind, fifth grade teacher, Mr. Larson, bringing Christmas presents for the whole family. That was the first time Jose really felt included in the fabric of this country.

He did well in school, graduated high school, went to college, and in 1987 found a hero, a champion. President Ronald Reagan granted amnesty to those immigrants who had made a good life here, followed the rules, and proved they were good citizens.

Peter Robinson, a former Reagan speechwriter, told NPR, "It was in Ronald Reagan's bones — it was part of his understanding of America — that the country was fundamentally open to those who wanted to join us here."

Jose raised his right hand, while his heart skipped a beat, and took an oath to become an American. Jose says it was one of the most amazing days of his life. His wife, Bonnie, and their two-year-old son, sat beside him. Little Joey is adorable, and he hugged everyone who took the oath. The memory still makes Jose laugh. That same memory, of Joey giving hugs, watching Jose being sworn in as an American citizen, brings tears.

That achievement, the feeling of safety for his family, of being included, is as precious as breath for Jose. Before that day he had to stand aside and watch as others voted, always feeling separated from the country he longed to be part of. He has never failed to vote since he became a citizen.

Jose, Bonnie, and their two children have discovered some of his extended family in Mexico and visit there every couple of years. They love many of the Mexican traditions, sharing them with his American extended family. There is never a family birthday without a piñata. His kindness, and gentle spirit, guides him, while he laughingly says, his wife makes most of the decisions. [3]

Jose makes sure his kids have all the things he never had. Yes, the material things, but more than that, they live with pride of being bi-cultural, without fear, or the feeling of being different. They have a beautiful home with enough land to accommodate a load of loved animals, both in the house, and in the back yard.

Jasmine, a haughty miniature Chihuahua, lounges on the back of the couch, and if let inside, Roman, a giant Bull Mastiff, flops on the kitchen floor and begs for belly rubs. Jose helped raise goats when he was small, loved them, and hated finding them on the table. Today he has two goats – their destiny – to keep the weeds down in the pasture. They would be *invited* to dinner, before they *became* dinner at this house. [4]

---

[3] A REAGAN Legacy: Amnesty For Illegal Immigrants : NPR*www.npr.or> News› History* Jul 4, 2010

Reflecting on his life, where he came from, and what he has accomplished, he told me, "I can't believe that this is really real, that my life, is my life. I am so fortunate."

Jose is humble. Being fortunate has little to do with his success. It is clear that he did it, he the master of his own life. He owns his own business, and is a great provider for his family, both financially and emotionally.

Jose and Bonnie are still smitten with each other, after 18 years. He and son, Joey, spend countless hours together, under the hood of classic cars; the paint job perfect, or riding horses in the mountains.

He is the proud Papa to Anne Marie, and glows when he talks about her, telling me all about her Quinceañera – her fifteenth birthday party, and ceremony, celebrating her transition to womanhood.

Above all else, Jose has time, patience, and caring, for all who find his door. He is the Pied Piper of goodness, a beautiful stitch in the fabric of America.

YOU ARE EXTRAORDINARY!

CONNIE TIMPSON

Part 3

Embolden Your Extraordinary

Say "Yes" To Your Extraordinary

There is one thing, or perhaps many, that you can do better than anyone else. Really. It does not need to be huge, to have a HUGE impact on yourself and others. Take a risk on yourself.

Let your *extraordinary* "wild child" out to play! Ignore the inner sound track that has been looping through all our minds since we were kids. You know the lyrics, "Do this – don't do that."

Our little, "written and recorded, just for us "ditty", played loudly. Its insistent, repetition overwhelmed us, back when we were supposed to be learning about the wonders of the world.

We should have been creating our own melody - back when we were "free range children", refusing to be totally programmed by society, and certainly, our parents.

Most of us listened too well. We packed up our curiosity, our dreams, our passions, our internal melody, and stuffed them all into a box. To make sure they did not get out – we used heavy-duty strapping tape and labeled the box before shoving it in the garage.

> *My Inner Extraordinary*
>
> *Keep it quiet.*
>
> *Keep it hidden.*
>
> *Leave this box alone!*

Go on! Find the box. Pull it out and rip off the tape. It will not hurt a bit. Pull back the flaps on the box and dig in.

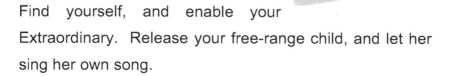

Find yourself, and enable your Extraordinary. Release your free-range child, and let her sing her own song.

Go On Color Outside The Lines
Take A Tip From Mary

Mary Phillips was raised to be a "Junior Leager", pearls and all. She went to the "right" schools, got an excellent education at a top university, graduated as a biologist, and married her college sweetheart. He got a job in Dallas.

Statuesque, blonde, and beautiful, she was destined to shop in high-end Dallas boutiques, and drink chardonnay, while letting the Brie breathe. But something was missing.

Mary was denying her inner extraordinary, her idealistic view of the world and the role her heart and soul wanted to play in it.

She had shelved her dreams of giving to the earth as it gives to us, or reclaiming used objects, and turning them into art. Her extraordinary view of the world was quieted.

Her dreams, however, were restless. They tried to sneak off the shelf, always whispering to her, nagging her creative right brain, begging her to let them come out of hiding.

The whispers turned into shouts and Mary finally tore the shelf down, broke it into pieces, and put a new life mosaic together. With determination, earth under her nails, and a lot of tears, Mary loosed her Extraordinary!

Where nothing grew in the Texas desert, Mary put down cardboard, mulch, a lot of love and precious seeds. In the hard packed, leached soil, nearly void of rain, she coaxed Eden to life.

She once told me that she wants to live to be very old, to live every minute of life to its fullest. She does!

Her creative brain is always engaged. Strapped in on a plane, pulling weeds, boxing up supplies for a company, for which she is the logistics V.P., she grabs for a scrap of paper, her plane ticket, or a piece of her, back to earth cardboard, and maniacally draws the new creation that has just popped into her head.

She, and husband Eddie, will then lovingly produce their creation from reclaimed parts of our world.

This creative, award-winning couple's sculptures, and murals, adorn much of the Fort Worth area.

Their aptly named "Guard'n Planet" Bohemian life – *works*.

Pieces like this *"Blue-Bottle Tree"* bring the earth, reclaimed parts of the world, and art together.

Mary's extraordinary brain is rarely quiet. She may be gathering pastel colored eggs from her free-range chickens, or changing the drip line on her completely organic garden, but she is also thinking about her organic life process, her imprint on this world.

Mary is aggravated by people who are unkind, but not by much else. A few months ago she was gathering eggs and reached under a hen only to have a huge Rat Snake bite her. (Non-poisonous, but still...) My response would have been to pass out!

Her inner biologist immediately surfaced. She grabbed the six-foot intruder, and pulled him out of the nest so he would not strangle a chicken, or eat the eggs. Then she posed for pictures, identified her naughty friend, cleaned her wound, and posted the pictures on face book! Seriously!

- *Compost?*

    Naturally.

- *Earth worms to enrich the soil?* (Raises them. Mary is happy to teach you how.)

What goodness she gleans from the earth goes into a pot, pan, or jar. If it is not eaten at her table it goes back into the earth from which Mary grew, and gathered it.

And did I tell you that this newly blended family has four kids, several cats, and three new Nigerian goats?

Of course Mary is planning to make her own Chèvre, just as soon as she learns how to help birth the "kids", milk the goats, and turn milk into cheese!

Mary colors her world the way she believes it should be colored - from the heart, without lines. Her only rule is:

> **Guard the planet, and make it richer,**
> **Honor it, tread lightly, and replant it.**

Mary has developed and perfected her
Inner, and Outer Extraordinary.

Embolden Your EXTRAordinary
It's a Right-Brain Thing

Understanding Your Amazing Noggin!

LEFT BRAIN FUNCTIONS

logical
detail driven
facts rule
words and language
reality based
strategizes
practical
conservative

RIGHT BRAIN FUNCTIONS

feeling
sees big picture
imagination rules
symbols & images
fantasy based
sees possibilities
impetuous
risk taker

The Right Side of the Brain helps you feel, create, and take risks. The right side is all about emotions, reactions, passion, and energy. It is where color inspires us, where we daydream, and *Imagination and Creativity rule.* It is where your *Extraordinary* is fueled and unfortunately, often stored, away from the light of the *serious* world.

The Left Side of the Brain is our Logic Center, Creating Balance. The left side looks at things analytically, helps us keep order of things, think logically, and helps us remember where on earth we put the keys! (It also helps reason that our Extraordinary should be kept quiet, out of the way of your logical life.)

The right side of your brain creates! It is where creativity lies dormant unless stimulated, prompted and used. (No, this is not a bunch of hooey, or junk science.) It is true. So the sooner you prompt the right side of your brain the sooner your Extraordinary can grow and take shape.

In the 1960's Roger Sperry and his colleagues did much research to determine which part of the brain does what.

They concluded that - the Right vision field is connected to the left hemisphere. Left vision field is connected to the right hemisphere.

Left-brain – logic.
Right-brain – emotions and creativity.

In the 1980's Sperry was awarded the Nobel Prize for Physiology. Even someone who was left-brained enough to solve complicated equations, was right-brained enough to *Imagine* there was much more to the brain and its functions than purely logical thought.

> *"The great pleasure and feeling in my right brain, is more than my left brain can find the words to tell you." Roger Sperry*

Yes, Sperry was *Extraordinary*, not because he became famous, but because he *"worked" his extraordinary.* His *extraordinary* helped catapult him to fame.

What Is Your Passion – Your Extraordinary?

Not, "What are you educated or trained to do" but "What makes your step a little lighter, your smile light your eyes? What makes you feel good about you?" (No, buying new shoes does not count. Even if they are red heels, or Fila Skele-Toes.)

---

[55] "The Split Brain Experiments". Nobelprize.org. 12 May 2012
http://www.nobelprize.org/educational/medicine/split-brain/background.html

What passion lies still, inside your inner you? Take a look. Call your passions from the shadows of your left brain. They are likely to be trapped under a load of debris.

Throw out the debris, the negative messages, and mind control from your cautious left side. Open your internal gate to your creative right side. Now run free! It is time to connect to your inner self. It's time your passion got noticed.

Often, it takes little more than the attitude of, "I can make someone else's day a little better, dust it with sparkles.

The Extraordinary Bye Bye

Yes, I had been up since 3 am to make my first flight, but I saw what I saw. At least I think so. Rolling toward the gate in gray-blue uniforms, and sensible-heeled pumps, the flight attendants giggled like girls going to the prom. Sparkling tiaras crowned two of their well-styled heads. What?

Two of the four gigglers not only wore tiaras but as they turned to grab the handles of their obligatory rolling bags I caught a flash of glittery sashes across their chests like "Queen Of The World."

Seriously.

They touched the flying castle's security-key pad; one set of red nails after the other and disappeared down the boarding ramp. Laughing, while I watched and wondered - what kind of flight was this?

My travel agent had assured me "I had plenty of time" to make my flight. *If I was Wonder Woman!*

I was exhausted. My lack of oxygen and tortured tootsies must have caused me to see things. Really.

I mean hallucinate. Like seeing flight attendants masquerading as beauty queens, or thinking I might get an open seat next to me, or at least not have to share the trans-Atlantic flight with a snoring seatmate. Right. Not a chance of that happening. I was relieved when I heard the snack cart coming. I was out of water.

"Could I get you some water?"

As I looked up from my book, a tiara-topped water-queen put the glass into my hand. I had not imagined it! There were two, beautiful, middle-aged black women handing out water, cokes, or compassion, smiling beneath tiaras and sparkling sashes. They said nothing about the prom, being in the Miss Queen Bee pageant, and no one questioned them. But they had a hint of "go ahead and ask humor in their eyes."

So I did…. the answer was a joyous smile.

With the flight closing in on Atlanta, an announcement broke the riddle on a ride that I felt would never end.

"Ladies and gentlemen, you may have noticed that two of our flight attendants are all dressed up today. It is their day to be treated like queens. After thirty-five years of extraordinary service they are retiring. When this plane touches down, their service to Delta ends. They are going to pass through the cabins and, if you would like, you can give them a little applause or words of congratulation."

Hand after hand came together, clapping, in support of these women, whom I am sure, had been puked on, coughed on, looked down upon, and grandly appreciated by others. Thirty-five years, I kept thinking. I couldn't even keep a bad habit thirty-five years!

Over three decades of missing school plays, weeks of sleep, and being able to toast your own bread. They had braved terrorist threats, turbulence, gate changes, cranky flyers, and grounded planes.

They stood erect. Smiling. Proud. I think proud, that we were proud of them. As we deplaned, they said their last bye-bye, shook hands with some, patted others, held on to a few.

As I worked my way toward the open door, I found myself beaming like a five year old at my first parade, proud of women who had broken the barriers.

I heard one person after another say, "thank you" in different languages, or accents. And I heard many "God bless." Whose God, it did not matter. At that moment there was no first class, zone one, or seventeen. There was no white, no black, no brown, no old, or new Europe, or no pro, or anti U.S. There was one class, and these extraordinary tiara-clad queens had brought us all together.

I passed the tiny one with dimples, , and I said, "Thank you," then I blurted, "You are beautiful. Thank you for being on this flight."

She touched her tiara, blushed, squeezed my hand and said, "I'm Maggie, honey. Thank you and bye, bye."

Extraordinary! Who can say that about an international flight? These women followed their Right Brain process, removed the left-brain filters, let their Extraordinary shine.... and wear tiaras!

Look To The Right – Please

Let the "Right Brain" process work for you to discover more of you, *your Extraordinary*. Don't over think it. Be totally honest about your passions, and complete these two simple statements: "I love to… or I would love to….

I Love To	I Would Love To

Prompt Your Creative Right Brain

Ask yourself what you really want, what you really care about. (Tell the left side to pipe down.) The right side needs to come out and "express itself."

- **Put up a virtual sticky -** Be bold, be greedy, it is time you spoke up for yourself.

- **Write up a paper sticky -** Stick it to the wall. Tape it to your bedroom ceiling. Wake to it, fall to sleep with it softly singing to you, just keep reaching toward your EXTRAordinary.

- **Color your inspiration -** Hang blocks of bold color around the room in which you think, write, or create. Use poster paper, fabric with different textures, and a favorite hat in your favorite color. Bold colors energize, empower, and inspire.

- **Record your thoughts.**
- **Write them down.**
- **Talk about your ideas.**
- **Take your idea for a run with a trusted colleague.**

Glean the best advice, observations, and compliments.

Negative responses – there's an app for that!
Make no judgments – simply write.

Jot down your ideas, loves, likes, wants, wishes. Scratch them onto a napkin, your kid's construction paper, whatever – *just write them down.* Writing them on the page is committing your belief in you. Your ideas become real, dimensional.

If a colleague asks you a question and you give him or her advice that they really liked – use it for yourself. Keep a Great Thoughts Account, Journal, or Stellar Thoughts Notebook. Now collect your great ideas and put them into a document you can easily access.

Let Your Right Brain Guide You To Your Inner EXTRAordinary

Without thinking about it, use your non-dominant hand and write about what makes you extraordinary. Yes, you can! It will free the creative part of you.

So, the pencil feels like you are wielding a tree! You will get used to it. It makes you give up a little control, to gain creativity and insight.

Using your non-dominant hand automatically connects you to your right brain functions. It removes the controls and filters that we have taken a lifetime to lock into place. It frees you to figure out who you really are, what magic lies inside, your dreams and passions.

The process picks the lock on your inner self, and lets it run free. Don't fret, the "left brain" controls are right there to help you drive your car, calculate your house payment or figure out just how far you ran this morning.

The process will free your mind and let you get to your unfiltered self. It is a direct line, to the real you - the one without filters, walls or boxes. It is the "unmanaged" you.

You will be surprised at what you read. It will come to you without filters, rules, or your own self-doubting whispers. It will come from your heart and mind.

What makes you different? Unique? What do you feel or think that is unusual? No inner critic, filters, or doubt allowed.

Your Daily Mantra

The more I believe in my own extraordinary, the more I will achieve.

The more I achieve, the more extraordinary I will become.

Affirming Your EXTRAordinary

I am EXTRAordinary because...

Intimidator - Step Off

Ignore the intimidators, the "detractors" the "naysayers" the ones who "have it all together." (They don't. Their left brain is in total control.) This is your quest.

He may be a bit bigger, outweigh you, but he cannot know what you know. He is no more talented, no smarter, or more creative than you are.

There is plenty of room for you on the playground. So move over big guy.

Some people know *some* things.
You know OTHER things.

Your experience and view of the world and how it works, is yours. It is unique. Let it empower and embolden you. Your experiences and learning in life are yours alone.

No one else has access to what you have stored away in your great Google - ish Brain.

Finding your passion – your inner extraordinary, is a freeing, empowering, feeling. It allows you to be more of *you,* the really good part of you. There are few who could be more true to who they really are, than our friend Malisa.

An EXTRAordinary Life in Constant Motion

Picture this – Christmas Day, five-year old twins, in-laws (both sides) husband's sister and family, neighbors, friends X 6, Shannon, the rescued German Shepherd that Barry and his dad drove 13 hours to adopt, mounds of wrapping paper, tons of food, eggnog, and 8 tiny pine trees all lighted, to guide Santa to the house. The word "Chaos" most likely comes to mind, but the real word is "Extraordinary" in every way.

Acceptance, inclusion, sharing the joy of their twins with all of us, laughter, stories, food, and did I say food? Lots of food.

Malisa is an orthopedic P.A. by education and training. More importantly, though, she is a humanitarian and wonder woman by heart and passion. She, and husband Barry, open their door to all whom they love, know, may be alone, those in need, and those who love them. And they are so easy to love.

YOU ARE EXTRAORDINARY!

Malisa went through nearly her entire pregnancy alone. Barry was in the Navy Reserve, stationed in Kuwait. Malisa didn't kvetch, snivel, or complain. She opened her heart. She invited my husband, Karl and me, inside her world, to be surrogate what-evers. There is no greater gift than to be included in this family.

We love being Aunt and Uncle, teacher of crafts, soccer, cookie decorating assistants, storytellers, and listeners of the world through the eyes of now five year-old's. Their imagination, and interpretation of life is amazing.

The twins are more than adorable and interesting! They are characters, like the Princess and the Rock Star. Yes, this is how they dressed for church. Mom and dad say, "That's how we roll." Meaning, they are each encouraged to develop their individual personality. These twins are as unalike as Princess Kate, and Mia Hamm - pure joy in our lives.

These two have only curiosity when more people appear at their table. Last year at Christmas we met two very nice Albanian people, Natasha and Sabin, who shared some of their traditions and holiday treats with the rest of us. One is a former engineer, the other a former journalist.

Now they are gardeners and house cleaners, and told us that they are glad of it. They both miss their professions, but feel rewarded by what America has given them. There is no fear of a knock on the door in the night, and jail for no reason.

Yes! What a discussion. This interesting couple cleans Malissa's house, and is welcome any time.

That same Christmas Day I was miserable with a foot problem. So while resting our over-stuffed bellies before over-stuffing them with dessert, Malissa gave me an individual present - cortisone in my foot on a day when she could have been tearing her hair out over the chaos, reposing on the couch, or worrying about whether the linen matched. (Linen at this house of love, is often paper and no one cares.) The important stuff is the big stuff, the good stuff, the Malisa Extraordinary soul stuff.

As a journalist, trainer and consultant I have had the good fortune of sharing time and space with some incredible people. I got an up-close look at Extraordinary, early on. One of the most extraordinary beings I have ever known was my mom. One of the hardest things I have ever done is let her go.

Hold The Extraordinary Close

Walking In The Light
of an Extraordinary Woman

When I least expect it, comes a missing so great that it takes my breath and sends me to my knees. I bite my knuckles trying to make the tears stop, and tell my best friend, my mother, that I miss her, love her, and…want her back. But God makes no deals. I have tried.

My Mom was a magnificent woman with dignity I can only dream of having. She never complained, never asked to be relieved of the pain that for over two years seized her organs and kept them hostage until they failed.

At her knee I learned to bake bread, sweeten yams – just enough, stitch a French knot into embroidery, set a perfect dam in the irrigation ditch to put water on the arid unforgiving land, drive the tractor, and appreciate the way the sun turned farmland pink and purple as it smiled on the day.

Dad was usually working away from home. If he was on the ranch he was busy catching up. The day-to-day "keep the ranch, and all the kids alive" fell onto my mom.

Even so, she was never too busy for any of her ten children.

When I was a Sr. in High School, my boyfriend of many years, dumped me two weeks before the prom. I cried all night, certain I would die by morning. Ignoring my shattered heart, the sun came up just like it did every morning. Mom tapped on my door, came in sat on the edge of the bed. She put her hand on my forehead, said I did not look like I felt very well, and that I should stay home with her. I did.

She took me to lunch in town, and asked no questions. Then she bought me a new pair of shoes. New shoes are so therapeutic! She did not want to know what happened. It did not matter. She knew the result. Mom simply waited for me to stop dying and try out my new red heels!

She was a great shrink, seamstress, helper of homework, cook, and ranch foreman.

Rising before the sun, she brought life to the land, watering it, tending it, willing it to provide. And before the sun broke through the clouds on the Butte, she had gathered eggs, made breakfast, and started a batch of mouth-watering bread.

As we grew older, we forgot that she grew even older. She still had spunk and energy. Until she didn't.

Only then did we tell ourselves the truth, something was seriously amiss. We made a decision, my three sisters, and me. We would be there, shuttle in and out, do our jobs half time, to take care of her like she had always taken care of us. It would be financially difficult, physically demanding, and some of the best years of my life.

Mornings were my favorite with Mom in her last two years. In the quiet, with the sun breaking night, we drank gallons of coffee, softly laughed, and pretended that we had lots of time. I started crocheting again. We did some embroidery.

We talked a lot. We laughed. And we cried.

We talked about her brother, my uncle Ralph, whose plane was shot down over France in the early days of WWII. We went through the picture box, retracing the paths of our family's life. Always, uncle Ralph's pictures were put back last.

Grandma believed that Ralph could run track faster if he had consumed a bowl of her delicious custard. I am sure it was true. He was a champion, and I have the simple, cherished, custard dish in my china cupboard.

No one knew where his final remains rested. Mom knew only that he would not return, and it left a giant hole in her heart. She told me it was like that for many families during those years that threatened to tear the world apart. There were too many people to notify, too many missing records, and too much pain. As my mom explained it – they were fighting a war, and had little time to attend to the details.

I could not leave this question unanswered. I made finding him a mad woman's quest. Two years of research, plowing through musty, partially burned military records in St. Louis, and finally I got an ID number from someone on line that knew the system. That number took me to a cemetery in St. Avold, France, on a cold snowy day.

I was stunned by the haunting beauty of the cemetery laid out like a giant cathedral in the forest. Row upon row, upon curved row of markers, created a tapestry of pain, of majesty, thankfullness, and perhaps closure for some.

It was a European holiday, so there was no one to ask for help, so I set out amid falling snow and a whipping wind. It is beautifully designed, but so huge it is overwhelming. I looked for his marker for hours. I had the row number, the marker number, but I walked until the snow covered every step I took. I felt my tears turn to ice. I thought about going back to the hotel, returning in the morning. I simply could not leave.

There had to be a system. I brushed snow off the bottom of one the markers and discovered the numbers. Finally, I figured out how the rows and marker numbers worked.

I burrowed through the snow until I could not feel my fingers, or my feet, my ears had long turned to stone. But it worked! I found his row and then his cross.

I finally lovingly, touched his name engraved on a single white cross among thousands. Amid blinding snow, I noticed Stars of David among the crosses. It seemed fitting that they all lie in that hallowed earth together, the protectors of freedom, who had given their "everything."

I could not wait to call Mom. I would write the story of searching and finally be able to tell my Mom, aunts and uncles where their brother lie. I have been back several times, but none were more joyous or heart breaking than the first.

It was worth every second - to put all of the pieces together. We read and re-read the story I wrote while searching for Uncle Ralph. It was a tiny thing to do for a woman who had given me so much. We shared it with my aunts and uncles, my Uncle Ralph's brothers and sisters. We all cried, but there was a tiny bit of closure.

Mom opened the secret spaces of her heart. She talked about her childhood, and told me stories that her mother had told her.

My ancestors came from the sturdy stock of men and women who boarded a ship in Liverpool, England and came to America, like many others, to pursue a dream.

Their dream was to get out of the dank, dirty and dangerous Welsh mines, and find religious freedom. They became part of America's handcart brigades. The sun tortured them. Skin that had rarely seen the sun, burned and blistered. The women wore bonnets with giant brims to avoid the sun's direct glare. The men wore hats as they pushed handcarts from Missouri to Salt Lake City.

More than 1,200 miles of terrain that had not felt a mountain goat touch its surface, much less people with carts.

We read many of their stories written as they ventured into a vast unknown. Grandmother Anna cried over leaving her china and delicately embroidered shawls. They buried her treasures, where they thought they would be safe until they could return for them. They never got back to their hidden treasure. Couldn't, just staying alive demanded all their attention.

There were Indian raids and keen hunger in their bellies, but the people from the handcart brigade were made of strong stuff, their hearts filled with determination.

My grandmother quoted them often,

"Tackle one mountain at a time."

It of course, means emotional mountains as well as rocks and spires.

On one occasion Utes rode into their tiny camp and demanded food in exchange for a child. (Most likely taken while raiding an enemy tribe.)

The century old writings say they then dropped the child like a discarded blanket; took the food, and rode away. The child was welcome in our family.

Some encounters with America's first people were deadly, terror filled. Many people of the handcart brigades were buried quickly, a prayer offered and tears held for another time.

One attack, we read, nearly cost my mother's great, great, grandmother, her life. She was scalped and left for dead on the trail. Luckily it rained and she rolled into a mud puddle, where mud stemmed the flow of blood. She was found by other brigades, nursed, and returned to her people.

She always wore what little bit of hair that remained, up in a knot on her head to cover the middle of her head where nothing grew. But she was alive.

Their dream was just one more mountain range away, another 500 miles, another few days with little to eat. Just one death-defying challenge after another. Walking. Always walking, mile after mile, mountain range after mountain range. Death after death. Mile after mile.

And not a decent pair of shoes among them.

I coaxed mom to retell the "I ran away with your dad and got married, two weeks after I met him" story. (I have heard tell that it was only 11 days, but you know how family stories go.)

My father had just returned from breaking the Japanese in WWII's most bloody battle - Okinawa – an experience that would haunt, and torture him, his entire, but short life. A Silver Star, or hero-worship made no difference.

A whirlwind romance took them to Helena, Montana and back, with vows of "forever." Mom once told me that there were no "forevers", sometimes not even "little whiles" – only "nows". She was absolutely right.

We talked about our immediate family's many shared losses. Tombstones mark the loss of four children, and two husbands.

We sometimes dared talk about the day that changed life for every member of my family.

Psychotic weather jerked my dad's plane from the sky and smashed it on the ground like a toy thrown by an angry child. It undid my Mom, left her in pieces, with a giant brood and no life insurance when she was in her mid 40's.

No one should bear so much pain. It was hard enough for me to lose my father, stepfather, three tiny sisters, and my hero oldest brother; but to bury your own child, four times, is unthinkable. Mom needed to say it, to talk about the unfairness, about giving so many back to God before she was ready to let them go.

But we also laughed – a lot.

We replayed the adventures of living on the ranch; watching cows walk over the telephone poles on hard-packed snow, my sister tricking me into jumping from a tree to catch a kitten that turned out to be a skunk!

We stuffed inner tubes into gunnysacks and floated the Snake River. (None of us knew how to swim. Luckily none of us is lying at the bottom of the river.) We made our own stage productions like a rendition of Swiss Family Robinson in a tree house that hung over the old-wood grainery.

I told her then that I had no idea how tired she must have been all of the time. She shrugged like, "It was my life."

I reminded her of the heavenly donuts she magically created in our chaotic kitchen. She ingeniously hung them on a wooden clothes rack, to let the glaze set. There are simply no donuts in the world like those created by my mom's hands. Ambrosia! (And yes, we lived in Idaho – they were spud-nuts.)

And what a sense of humor! Even when she was very ill. One afternoon I got her out of her new-fangled electric lounger, helped her into her wheelchair, and pushed her into the bathroom. While helping her out of the wheelchair and onto the toilet, I lost my balance and practically sat in her lap.

Instead of panicking, or complaining, she used her ever-ready dry wit and said, "I'm sorry, Connie, you will have to wait your turn. This seat is taken."

Indeed the seat was taken, with one of God's favorite children.

When we were little there was a "no animals in the house policy" but over time Mom opened her door to strays, whether it was an animal, or a child in need. To know my mom was to know love, acceptance, and great food.

When the time came, it was devastating, though doctors had told us to expect it for a very long time. Letting go of this extraordinary woman is the most difficult thing I have ever done.

She knew we loved her, told her, told her, and told her. And she told us that she loved us, that in her final years, we had given back more than she had given to us in all our growing up.

It was the only lie she ever told.

This extraordinary woman gave me the strength to believe that each of us has something special, that we are a sum of our life experiences, and the people who love us, stay with us forever. I look into the mirror and try to find bits of her in me. I see them in my sisters.

If every child could live in the radiance of a woman with such extraordinary insight, courage, and quiet dignity, the world would be a better, richer, far more livable place.

She was an incredible package of EXTRAordinary

CONNIE TIMPSON